SCIENCE
THE SCIENCE OF
SOCCER

EMILY MAHONEY

PowerKiDS
press.

New York

Published in 2016 by The Rosen Publishing Group, Inc.
29 East 21st Street, New York, NY 10010

First Edition

Editor: Katie Kawa
Book Design: Katelyn Heinle

Photo Credits: Cover, p. 13 Fotokostic/Shutterstock.com; back cover kubais/Shutterstock.com; p. 5 © iStockphoto.com/monkeybusinessimages; p. 7 muzsy/Shutterstock.com; p. 9 (soccer ball) Oris Arisara/Shutterstock.com; p. 9 (Brazuca) stepmorem/Shutterstock.com; p. 10 gualtiero boffi/Shutterstock.com; p. 11 tazik13/Shutterstock.com; pp. 14, 17 (vector soccer players) My Life Graphic/Shutterstock.com; p. 15 Hector Vivas/STR/LatinContent WO/Getty Images; p. 17 (David Beckham) ROBYN BECK/AFP/Getty Images; p. 19 © iStockphoto.com/isitsharp; p. 21 (goalie) Copa Euroamericana/CON/LatinContent Editorial/Getty Images; p. 21 (football player) Tacoma News Tribune/Tribune News Service/Getty Images; p. 21 (soccer player) AFP/Getty Images; p. 21 (hockey player) Jamie Sabau/Getty Images Sport/Getty Images; p. 23 Jakkrit Orrasri/Shutterstock.com; pp. 24, 25 YASUYOSHI CHIBA/AFP/Getty Images; p. 26 http://upload.wikimedia.org/wikipedia/commons/1/16/Wembley_Stadium_interior.jpg; p. 27 John Lamb/Photographer's Choice/Getty Images; p. 29 Vladimir Melnik/Shutterstock.com; p. 30 © iStockphoto.com/strickke.

Library of Congress Cataloging-in-Publication Data

Mahoney, Emily Jankowski, author.
 The science of soccer / Emily Mahoney.
    pages cm. — (Sports science)
 Includes bibliographical references and index.
 ISBN 978-1-4994-1071-6 (pbk.)
 ISBN 978-1-4994-1108-9 (6 pack)
 ISBN 978-1-4994-1148-5 (library binding)
1. Soccer—Equipment and supplies—Juvenile literature. 2. Soccer—Miscellanea—Juvenile literature. I. Title.
 GV943.9.E65M34 2016
 796.334—dc23
                        2015006118

Manufactured in the United States of America

CPSIA Compliance Information: Batch #WS15PK: For Further Information contact Rosen Publishing, New York, New York at 1-800-237-9932

CONTENTS

EXCITING SCIENCE!

Soccer is one of the most popular sports in the world, and its popularity is growing quickly in the United States. Soccer's popularity is growing because it's such an exciting game. From the speed of a corner kick to "bending it like Beckham" to score a goal, the sport of soccer is certainly action-packed!

How do players know how to kick the ball to hit the back of the net? How does the equipment, or gear, the players wear affect their game? We can answer these questions and more using science. Athletes who play soccer must be very fit and healthy. Understanding the science behind training for and playing in a soccer game helps them be their best on the field.

"Soccer" is the word used in the United States to describe this sport, but it's called "football" in other countries.

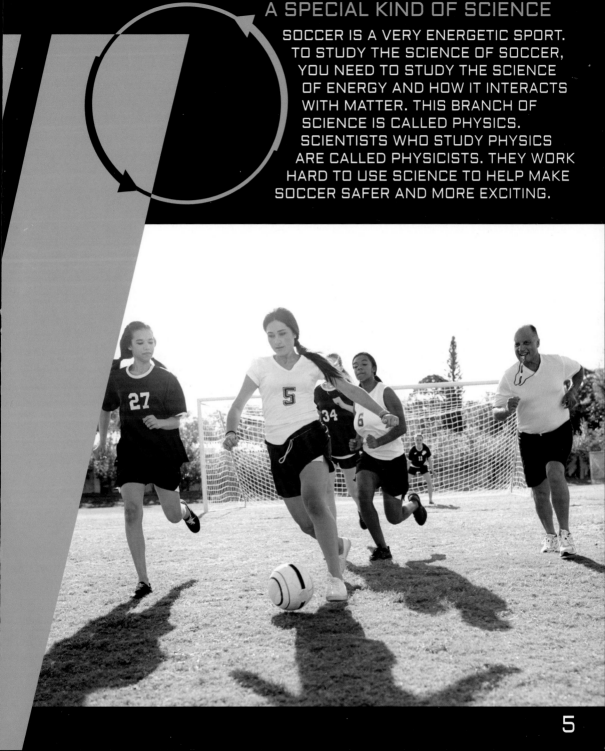

A SPECIAL KIND OF SCIENCE

SOCCER IS A VERY ENERGETIC SPORT. TO STUDY THE SCIENCE OF SOCCER, YOU NEED TO STUDY THE SCIENCE OF ENERGY AND HOW IT INTERACTS WITH MATTER. THIS BRANCH OF SCIENCE IS CALLED PHYSICS. SCIENTISTS WHO STUDY PHYSICS ARE CALLED PHYSICISTS. THEY WORK HARD TO USE SCIENCE TO HELP MAKE SOCCER SAFER AND MORE EXCITING.

Physicists study forces and motion, and examples of both can be seen throughout a soccer game. A force is a push or pull **exerted** on an object. Motion can be seen as soccer players run all over the field. However, not all motion in a soccer game is the same, so it needs to be measured differently.

Speed measures the rate at which something moves. The direction an object moves doesn't matter when measuring speed. For example, a soccer player can show speed when they run even if they end up back where they started on the field.

Velocity measures the rate at which something changes its position, so the direction of movement matters. To show velocity, an object needs to move away from where it started. A soccer player can show this by running down the field to score a goal.

This chart shows some of the forces that can be seen in action during a soccer game.

ACCELERATE!

ACCELERATION IS ANOTHER WAY MOTION IS MEASURED. IT'S THE MEASUREMENT OF HOW MUCH AN OBJECT'S VELOCITY CHANGES OVER TIME. WHEN VELOCITY INCREASES, THE OBJECT IS SAID TO BE ACCELERATING. A SOCCER PLAYER ACCELERATES WHEN THEY INCREASE THEIR VELOCITY TO MOVE FASTER THAN THE **DEFENDERS** AROUND THEM IN ORDER TO REACH THE GOAL.

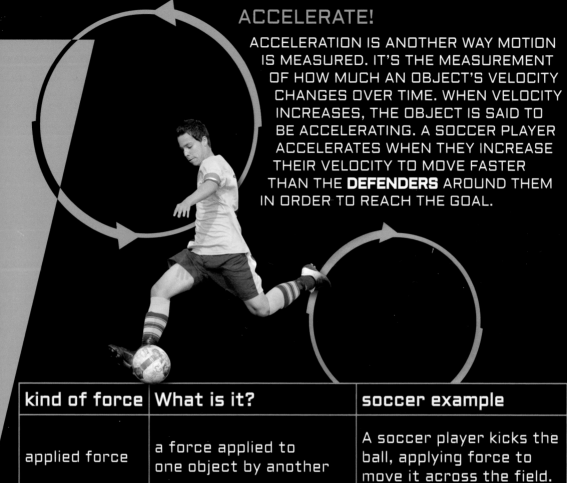

kind of force	What is it?	soccer example
applied force	a force applied to one object by another	A soccer player kicks the ball, applying force to move it across the field.
gravity force	the force that pulls objects to Earth	When a soccer ball is kicked into the air, the force of gravity makes it come back down to the ground.
friction force	a force exerted when one object tries to move across a surface	Friction exists between a rolling soccer ball and the surface of the field. That's why the ball slows down and stops.

The specific shape of a soccer ball is a truncated icosahedron, which is a shape with 60 vertices, or points. Soccer balls commonly have 12 pentagonal (five-sided) faces and 20 hexagonal (six-sided) faces. Each face is stitched or glued on as its own patch, or panel. These faces are curved, so the ball has a shape close to a sphere.

Scientists have experimented with the number of panels that the ball is made from. Wind tunnel tests and robotic kickers have been used in these experiments. These tests often compare the aerodynamics of different kinds of soccer balls. Aerodynamics is a branch of science that studies the way air moves around objects and the way objects, such as soccer balls, move through the air.

Traditional soccer balls are commonly black and white. The pentagons are black, and the hexagons are white. Some newer soccer balls, such as the Brazuca, are many colors.

EXTRA POINT

"Brazuca" is a term commonly used to express national pride in Brazil, which was the country where the 2014 World Cup was held. The Brazuca soccer ball is made of six panels instead of 32.

SOCCER BALL

BRAZUCA

LOOKING WITH LASERS

THE SOCCER BALL USED IN THE 2014 FIFA WORLD CUP WAS CALLED THE BRAZUCA, AND IT WAS TESTED IN A WIND TUNNEL THAT USED SMOKE AND LASERS TO STUDY ITS AERODYNAMICS. LASERS ARE DEVICES THAT PRODUCE NARROW BEAMS OF LIGHT. THE LASERS SHOWED CHANGES IN THE WAY THE SMOKE MOVED AROUND THE BALL.

A soccer ball is more scientific than just the number of shapes on its surface. Air pressure also factors into the effectiveness of a soccer ball. Even though air **molecules** are invisible, they still have weight and take up space. The force of these air molecules pressing against an object or surface is air pressure.

Air pressure is created inside a container, or an object used to hold something, when air molecules get crammed together in one place. A soccer ball is a container because it holds air. A soccer ball has air molecules pumped into its center, which is a rubber **bladder**. The air pressure inside the ball increases as more air is pumped into the ball.

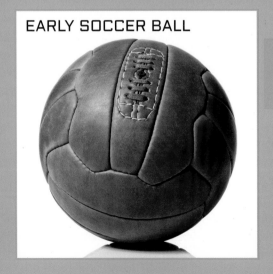

EARLY SOCCER BALL

EXTRA POINT
In the 1800s, soccer balls used to be made of pig or ox bladders covered in leather.

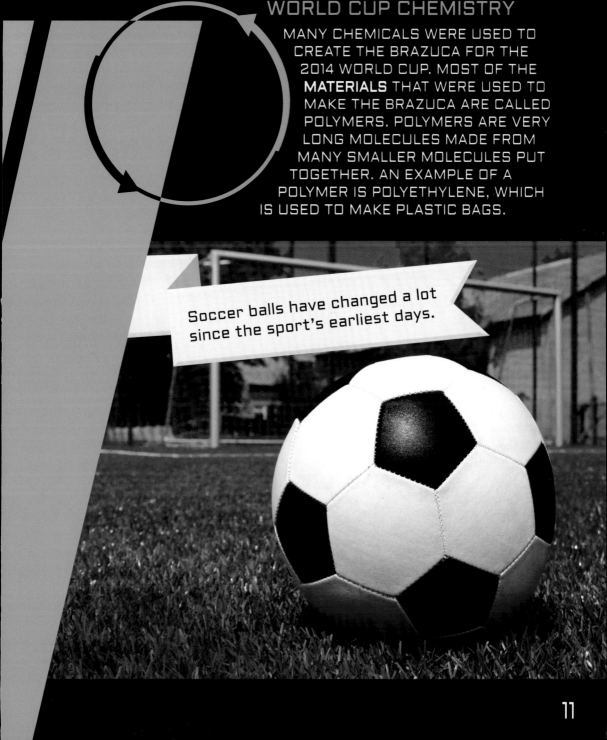

WORLD CUP CHEMISTRY

MANY CHEMICALS WERE USED TO CREATE THE BRAZUCA FOR THE 2014 WORLD CUP. MOST OF THE **MATERIALS** THAT WERE USED TO MAKE THE BRAZUCA ARE CALLED POLYMERS. POLYMERS ARE VERY LONG MOLECULES MADE FROM MANY SMALLER MOLECULES PUT TOGETHER. AN EXAMPLE OF A POLYMER IS POLYETHYLENE, WHICH IS USED TO MAKE PLASTIC BAGS.

Soccer balls have changed a lot since the sport's earliest days.

Science can be used to figure out the best way to kick a soccer ball. A common saying in soccer is: "If you kick with your toe, who knows where it goes!" Soccer players actually kick the ball with the instep, or side, of their foot. This gives the player more control over the direction of the ball than kicking with the toe. This is because the instep has a greater surface area than the toe.

When kicking a soccer ball, a player starts by approaching the ball from the side. This allows the hip to rotate, or turn, which creates more foot speed and force to move the ball. Hips can rotate because they're joints, which are body parts where bones come together.

Soccer players want to create as much force as possible when they kick the ball, especially if they're taking a shot or making a long pass.

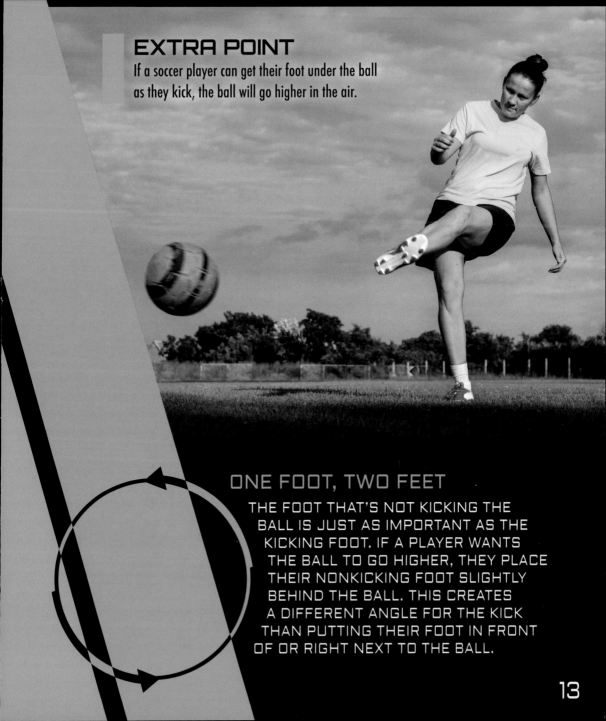

EXTRA POINT

If a soccer player can get their foot under the ball as they kick, the ball will go higher in the air.

ONE FOOT, TWO FEET

THE FOOT THAT'S NOT KICKING THE BALL IS JUST AS IMPORTANT AS THE KICKING FOOT. IF A PLAYER WANTS THE BALL TO GO HIGHER, THEY PLACE THEIR NONKICKING FOOT SLIGHTLY BEHIND THE BALL. THIS CREATES A DIFFERENT ANGLE FOR THE KICK THAN PUTTING THEIR FOOT IN FRONT OF OR RIGHT NEXT TO THE BALL.

CORNER KICKS

A corner kick is an important part of soccer, and it occurs when a team knocks the ball out of bounds on the goal line they're defending. These kicks can be tricky because they're taken from the corner of the field and many players are in the area where the ball usually lands.

There are two types of corner kicks: inswinging and outswinging. An inswinging kick curves outward from the goal line and then comes back in. It's useful because the trajectory of the ball places it closer to the net. An outswinging kick curves the ball in towards the goal line and then away from the goal. It's more difficult for the goalie to save, but also moves the ball farther from the net.

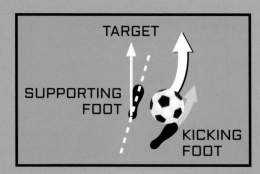

Corner kicks can be confusing for goalies because the ball's trajectory can change as it's moving very quickly.

PEOPLE WHO ANALYZE, OR STUDY, SOCCER OFTEN WANT TO KNOW HOW LIKELY IT IS THAT A CORNER KICK WILL LEAD TO A GOAL. TO FIND THIS OUT, THEY NEED TO USE A KIND OF MATH CALLED PROBABILITY. THE PROBABILITY OF SCORING ON A CORNER KICK IS THE **RATIO** OF TIMES A GOAL IS SCORED ON A CORNER KICK TO THE TOTAL NUMBER OF CORNER KICKS TAKEN.

EXTRA POINT

The trajectory of a soccer ball is the path it follows while in the air.

BENDING IT LIKE BECKHAM

David Beckham is famous for his skill at "bending" a soccer ball's trajectory around players to score. This skill actually has a scientific name: the Magnus effect.

The Magnus effect is caused by changes in velocity as an object moves through a liquid or gas, such as air. In soccer, the Magnus effect can be seen when a spinning soccer ball moves through the air. The resistance, or drag, caused by the air around the ball slows the movement of the air on one side of the ball and speeds up the air's movement on the opposite side. This causes a difference in air pressure, and the ball bends its trajectory toward the lower air pressure on the side where the air is moving faster.

THE MAGNUS EFFECT IN OTHER SPORTS

THE MAGNUS EFFECT IS SEEN IN MANY OTHER SPORTS, TOO. IF A BALL IS SPINNING THROUGH THE AIR, YOU'LL BE ABLE TO SEE THE MAGNUS EFFECT IN ACTION. IN BASEBALL, THE MAGNUS EFFECT IS THE REASON CURVEBALL PITCHES CURVE. GOLFERS USE THE MAGNUS EFFECT TO BEND THEIR SHOTS AROUND THINGS THAT ARE IN THEIR WAY, SUCH AS TREES.

EXTRA POINT

The way a soccer ball's path curves when the Magnus effect is at work is commonly called a "banana kick" because the trajectory is curved like a banana.

It takes a lot of skill and a lot of science to bend it like Beckham!

Soccer players generally aren't allowed to use their hands. Heading the ball is an important part of a soccer game because it allows players to direct the ball while it's still in the air. However, it can also be dangerous. Generally, it's recommended that players hit the ball with their forehead, not the top of their head. This lessens the likelihood of headache or brain **injury** because the forehead is a thicker part of the skull.

Neuroscientists, or scientists who study the brain, say players should be very careful when heading the ball. If you feel dizzy, have a headache or blurry vision, or feel sick to your stomach after heading a ball, go to the sidelines to be checked out by a trainer or coach. These are all signs of a concussion, which is a serious head injury.

Knowing how to head the ball correctly can save you from serious head injuries. It can also help you score a goal!

HEADING FOR TROUBLE?

CONCUSSIONS MAKE UP ABOUT 3 PERCENT OF ALL SOCCER-RELATED INJURIES. MOST INJURIES IN SOCCER (UP TO 80 PERCENT) ARE TO THE LEGS AND FEET. HOWEVER, HEAD INJURIES CAN BE VERY DANGEROUS, DESPITE THEIR SMALL PERCENTAGE. MEMORY LOSS IS ONE OF MANY LONG-TERM PROBLEMS PEOPLE MIGHT DEAL WITH AFTER GETTING A CONCUSSION.

EXTRA POINT

Neuroscientists are also studying the effects of other sports, such as hockey and football, on the human brain.

Soccer players are now allowed to wear headgear to prevent concussions. These headbands or helmets help to **absorb** the impact that can come from heading the ball or getting hit in the head by another player. Although they're not required, some players choose to wear them to lessen the injuries that can result from a hard hit.

Players are, however, required to wear shin guards to keep their lower legs from being injured. Shin guards are made to prevent a broken tibia, which is the large bone in the leg near the shin. In one study, the force of the impact from a kick to the tibia was reduced by nearly 20 percent by wearing shin guards.

GOALIE GLOVES

GOALIES ARE THE ONLY PLAYERS ON A SOCCER FIELD WHO USE THEIR HANDS THROUGHOUT THE GAME. THEY USE THEIR HANDS TO BLOCK SHOTS AND CATCH BALLS KICKED IN THEIR DIRECTION. BECAUSE THEIR HANDS ARE SO IMPORTANT, THEY OFTEN WEAR SPECIAL GLOVES. THESE GLOVES ARE MADE TO INCREASE FRICTION BETWEEN A GOALIE'S HANDS AND THE BALL, HELPING THEM MAKE MORE SAVES.

Most soccer players wear socks that go up to their knees. These socks help keep their shin guards in place.

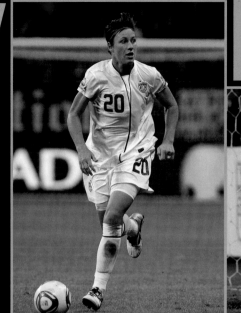

HOCKEY

FOOTBALL

Soccer players don't wear as much safety equipment as athletes who play hockey or football. However, the gear they do wear is important because it helps prevent common soccer injuries.

TRAINING FOR THE GAME

Part of the science behind the game of soccer comes from the way players train to be in the best shape possible for each game. Recently, a type of training called plyometrics has become popular because of its success. Plyometrics involves exercises, such as jumping, that quickly stretch and contract muscles. Stretching makes muscles longer, and contracting shortens them. Doing exercises that stretch and contract muscles increases muscle power.

EXTRA POINT

A soccer player can run as many as 7 miles (11.2 km) during a soccer game.

SNACK ATTACK!

ALL ATHLETES MUST BE ESPECIALLY AWARE OF THE FOOD THEY EAT. SOCCER PLAYERS NEED TO EAT A LOT OF COMPLEX CARBOHYDRATES BECAUSE THEY GIVE THE PLAYERS ENERGY FOR A LONG PERIOD OF TIME. COMPLEX CARBOHYDRATES OFTEN COME FROM PLANTS, INCLUDING BEANS, VEGETABLES, AND GRAINS. WHOLE-GRAIN FOODS GIVE ATHLETES A LOT OF ENERGY.

Endurance training is also important for soccer players. This kind of training helps soccer players run for long and short distances over long periods of time. Since soccer is a 90-minute game played with few breaks, it's important for players to be able to remain strong and fast for the whole game.

Soccer players also need to drink a lot of water. They sweat a lot, and drinking water puts the water ~~~ through sweating back into their body.

Soccer players use a lot of energy as they run across the field. The energy soccer players have when they run is kinetic energy. Kinetic energy is energy an object has by being in motion, or energy being used to do work.

Energy can't be created or destroyed, but it can change forms. This is the basis for the law of **conservation** of energy. It's also the basis for an idea Brazilian engineers had for a new soccer field. This field, which opened in 2014, uses panels beneath the grass to harness the kinetic energy of the players. This kinetic energy is then used to power the field's lights. Kinetic energy is changed to light energy to allow soccer games to continue after dark.

Pelé, one of the most famous Brazilian soccer players of all time, visited the first player-powered soccer field on its opening day.

SOLAR PANELS

BRAZIL'S PLAYER-POWERED SOCCER FIELD DOESN'T GET ALL ITS ELECTRICAL POWER FROM KINETIC ENERGY. IT ALSO USES SOLAR PANELS. THESE PANELS HARNESS ENERGY FROM THE SUN. THIS ENERGY WORKS WITH THE KINETIC ENERGY OF THE PLAYERS TO PRODUCE ENOUGH POWER TO MAKE THE FIELD'S LIGHTS TURN ON. SOLAR PANELS ARE USED AROUND THE WORLD TO TURN ENERGY FROM THE SUN INTO ELECTRICITY.

PLAYER-POWERED SOCCER FIELD
MINEIRA FAVELA, RIO DE JANEIRO, BRAZIL

EXTRA POINT

Tiles used to harness kinetic energy can also be found in European airports and train stations, as well as shopping malls in Australia.

Soccer can be played anywhere, but the best soccer players in the world play in huge **stadiums**. Engineers use math and science to build soccer stadiums. One of the most impressive soccer stadiums is located in England. Wembley Stadium has a retractable roof, which means it can open and close. The roof is supported by a 170-foot (51.8 m) arch. The arch was built so no **pillars** were needed to hold up the roof, which would have blocked some views of the field for fans. The arch, with its span of 1,033 feet (315 m), is the longest single-span roof structure in the world!

Wembley Stadium seats over 90,000 people and was opened in 2007. It's the stadium that the England national soccer team calls home.

EXTRA POINT

Wembley Stadium has a circumference of 0.62 mile (1 km). The circumference is the distance around the outside edge of the circular stadium.

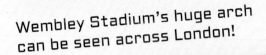
Wembley Stadium's huge arch can be seen across London!

THE BEST OF BOTH WORLDS

THE FIELD AT WEMBLEY STADIUM IS MADE OF A SPECIAL COMBINATION OF REAL GRASS AND MAN-MADE GRASS CALLED ARTIFICIAL TURF. THIS ALLOWS THE FIELD TO BE MORE DURABLE, OR STRONGER, THAN A GRASS FIELD. IN FACT, THE FIELD AT WEMBLEY STADIUM WAS MADE TO BE DURABLE ENOUGH TO HOST SOCCER GAMES, AMERICAN FOOTBALL GAMES, AND MUSIC CONCERTS.

Soccer fans love vuvuzelas—plastic horns that are blown at games to add to the noise and excitement. However, FIFA, the group that governs soccer worldwide, has banned the horns from World Cup games. The horns are so loud they were bothering the players. Vuvuzelas are also able to produce sounds loud enough to cause pain. They were hurting other fans' ears and keeping them from enjoying the games.

A vuvuzela works like all horns. A person blows air into it, creating sound waves that produce a certain pitch. A sound's pitch is how high or low it is. Pitch is determined by the sound wave's frequency, or the number of times the wave is repeated over a certain period. When a person changes how much air they blow into the vuvuzela, its sound can change.

The vuvuzela can produce sounds up to 127 decibels. That's louder than a clap of thunder!

LOUD CROWDS

SOCCER FANS ARE AMONG THE LOUDEST SPORTS FANS IN THE WORLD! SOCCER FANS AT THE TURK TELEKOM ARENA IN TURKEY HELD THE RECORD FOR THE LOUDEST CROWD IN A STADIUM UNTIL 2013, WHEN FANS OF THE NATIONAL FOOTBALL LEAGUE'S SEATTLE SEAHAWKS BROKE THEIR RECORD. THE SOUND FROM THE CROWD AT TURK TELEKOM ARENA ONCE REACHED OVER 131 DECIBELS. A DECIBEL, OR DB, IS A UNIT USED TO MEASURE HOW LOUD SOMETHING IS.

EXTRA POINT

The current record for the loudest sports fans in a stadium is held by fans of the National Football League's Kansas City Chiefs. In 2014, they created a roar of 142.2 decibels.

Soccer is even more exciting when you know the science behind it. The game is influenced not only by players' abilities, but by many scientific forces as well, including air pressure, friction, and drag. Smart soccer players know how to use science to help their team win.

You can use what you've learned from this book to improve your soccer skills. Using the proper gear, knowing about friction, and learning how to bend your kicks will make you a better player overall. Maybe one day you'll be a star soccer player, leading your teammates and scoring with science.

GLOSSARY

absorb: To take in.

bladder: A sac in an animal's body that holds fluids; also, a soft bag filled with water or air.

conservation: The act of keeping a constant amount of something during a process of change.

defender: A player in a sport whose job is to stop another player or team from scoring.

exert: To put forth.

injury: Harm or damage done to the body.

material: Something from which something else can be made.

molecule: The smallest part of something.

pillar: A large post that helps hold up something.

ratio: The relationship between two things that is often represented by numbers.

stadium: A large, commonly outdoor building where people gather to watch sporting events.

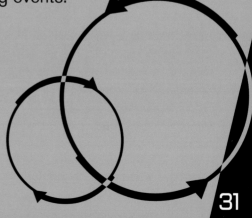

INDEX

WEBSITES

Due to the changing nature of Internet links, PowerKids Press has developed an online list of websites related to the subject of this book. This site is updated regularly. Please use this link to access the list: www.powerkidslinks.com/spsci/socc